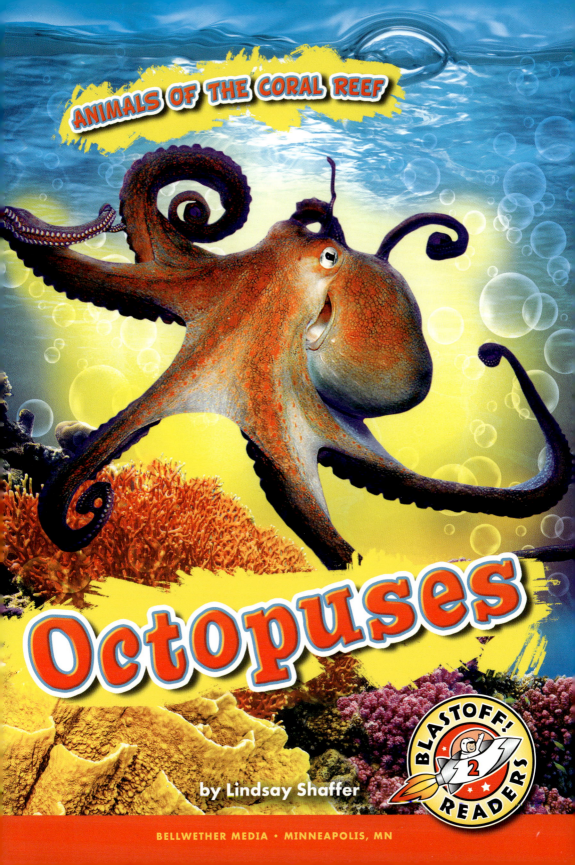

Note to Librarians, Teachers, and Parents:

Blastoff! Readers are carefully developed by literacy experts and combine standards-based content with developmentally appropriate text.

Level 1 provides the most support through repetition of high-frequency words, light text, predictable sentence patterns, and strong visual support.

Level 2 offers early readers a bit more challenge through varied simple sentences, increased text load, and less repetition of high-frequency words.

Level 3 advances early-fluent readers toward fluency through increased text and concept load, less reliance on visuals, longer sentences, and more literary language.

Level 4 builds reading stamina by providing more text per page, increased use of punctuation, greater variation in sentence patterns, and increasingly challenging vocabulary.

Level 5 encourages children to move from "learning to read" to "reading to learn" by providing even more text, varied writing styles, and less familiar topics.

Whichever book is right for your reader, Blastoff! Readers are the perfect books to build confidence and encourage a love of reading that will last a lifetime!

This edition first published in 2020 by Bellwether Media, Inc.

No part of this publication may be reproduced in whole or in part without written permission of the publisher. For information regarding permission, write to Bellwether Media, Inc., Attention: Permissions Department, 6012 Blue Circle Drive, Minnetonka, MN 55343.

Library of Congress Cataloging-in-Publication Data

Names: Shaffer, Lindsay, author.
Title: Octopuses / by Lindsay Shaffer.
Description: Minneapolis, MN : Bellwether Media, Inc., 2020. | Series: Animals of the coral reef | Includes bibliographical references and index. | Audience: Ages 5-8 | Audience: Grades K-1 |
  Summary: "Relevant images match informative text in this introduction to octopuses. Intended for students in kindergarten through third grade"-- Provided by publisher.
Identifiers: LCCN 2019033053 (print) | LCCN 2019033054 (ebook) | ISBN 9781644871331 (library binding) | ISBN 9781618918154 (ebook)
Subjects: LCSH: Octopuses--Juvenile literature.
Classification: LCC QL430.3.O2 S527 2020 (print) | LCC QL430.3.O2 (ebook) | DDC 594/.56--dc23
LC record available at https://lccn.loc.gov/2019033053
LC ebook record available at https://lccn.loc.gov/2019033054

Text copyright © 2020 by Bellwether Media, Inc. BLASTOFF! READERS and associated logos are trademarks and/or registered trademarks of Bellwether Media, Inc.

Editor: Betsy Rathburn   Designer: Laura Sowers

Printed in the United States of America, North Mankato, MN.

Table of Contents

Life in the Coral Reef	4
Escape Plans	12
Hidden Hunters	16
Glossary	22
To Learn More	23
Index	24

Life in the Coral Reef

common octopus

Octopuses are **cephalopods**. They live in oceans all around the world.

Many have **adapted** to the coral reef **biome**.

Common Octopus Range

range =

Coral reefs are full of **predators**. Octopuses must find places to hide.

They look for cracks in the reef. Their soft bodies easily squeeze inside!

Octopuses hide using **camouflage**. Their skin changes color. It may look more bumpy or smooth.

Special Adaptations

eight arms

soft body

sharp beak

Octopuses may look like rocks, **coral**, or seaweed!

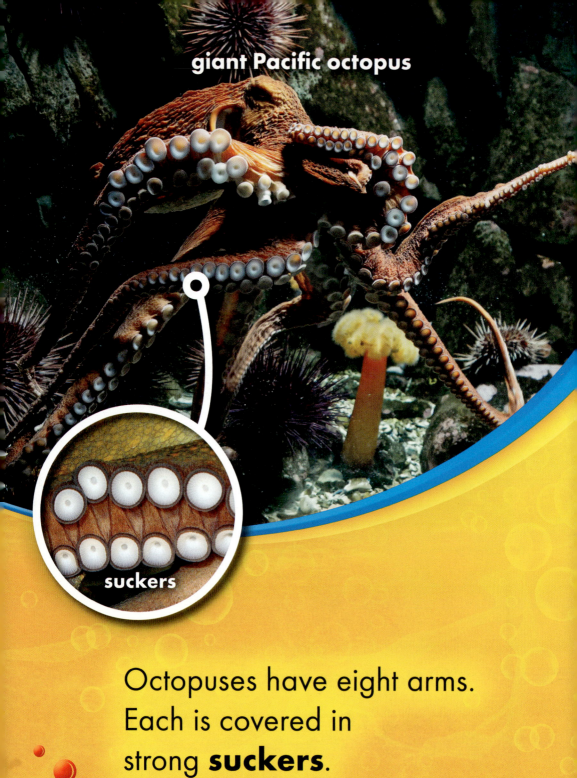

giant Pacific octopus

suckers

Octopuses have eight arms. Each is covered in strong **suckers**.

Octopuses use their arms to explore coral reefs. The arms can grab, smell, and taste!

Escape Plans

Octopuses face many dangers in coral reefs.

They escape bites by dropping an arm. They later grow a new one!

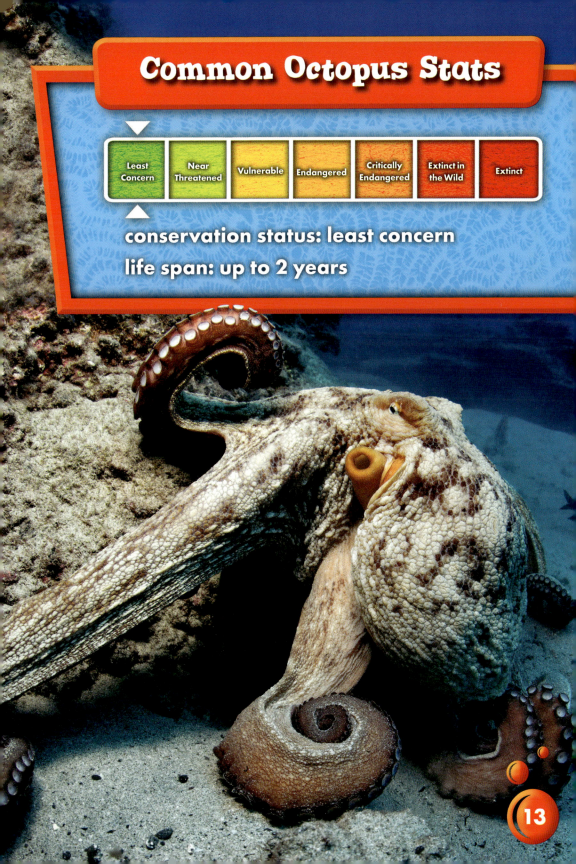

Common Octopus Stats

| Least Concern | Near Threatened | Vulnerable | Endangered | Critically Endangered | Extinct in the Wild | Extinct |

conservation status: least concern

life span: up to 2 years

ink →

Octopuses have other ways to escape, too. They blast predators with ink.

The confused attackers cannot see or smell. Octopuses swim away safely!

Hidden Hunters

Caribbean reef octopus

Octopuses are sneaky hunters. They wait for **prey** to come close.

Suddenly, they strike! Their arms and suckers keep prey from escaping.

Octopus mouths have sharp beaks. They easily break through shells!

Octopus Diet

red king crabs

mantis shrimp

tiger tail sea cucumbers

Then the octopus releases **venom** to weaken prey.

Octopuses like to hunt at night. Their long arms search for prey inside the reef.

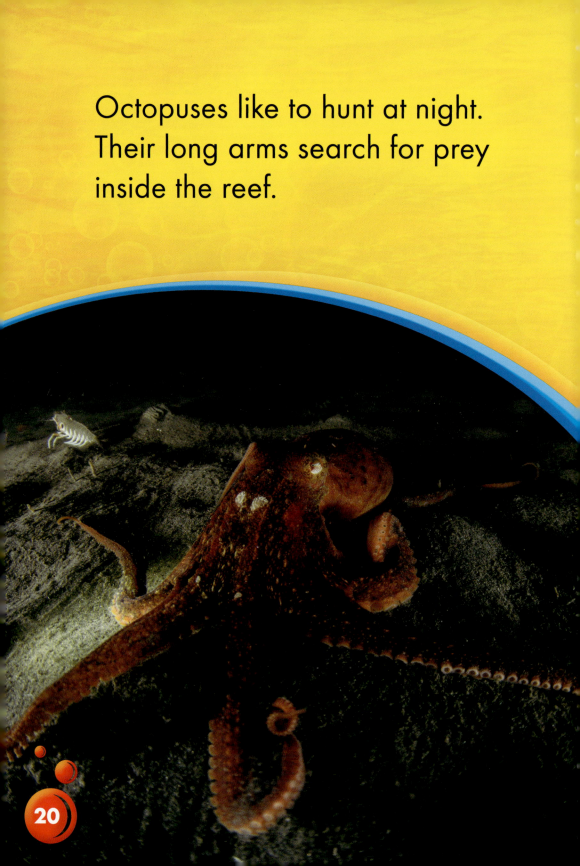

These **carnivores** find a lot to eat in the coral reef biome!

Glossary

adapted—changed over a long period of time

biome—a large area with certain plants, animals, and weather

camouflage—coloring or markings that make animals look like their surroundings

carnivores—animals that only eat meat

cephalopods—animals that have excellent eyesight, ink sacs, and muscular arms with suckers

coral—a hard material formed from the skeletons of small animals

predators—animals that hunt other animals for food

prey—animals that are hunted by other animals for food

suckers—the round parts of octopus arms that stick to prey

venom—poison produced by an animal

To Learn More

AT THE LIBRARY
Drimmer, Stephanie Warren. *Ink!* Washington, D.C.: National Geographic Kids, 2019.

Gaertner, Meg. *Mimic Octopuses*. North Mankato, Minn.: Capstone Press, 2020.

Hulick, Kathryn. *Coral Reefs*. New York, N.Y.: AV2 by Weigl, 2019.

ON THE WEB

Factsurfer.com gives you a safe, fun way to find more information.

1. Go to www.factsurfer.com.
2. Enter "octopuses" into the search box and click 🔍.
3. Select your book cover to see a list of related web sites.

Index

adaptations, 5, 9
arms, 9, 10, 11, 12, 17, 20
beaks, 9, 18
biome, 5, 21
bodies, 7, 9
camouflage, 8
carnivores, 21
cephalopods, 4
color, 8
coral, 9
cracks, 7
eat, 21
escape, 12, 14, 17
hide, 6, 8
hunters, 16, 20
ink, 14
mouths, 18
night, 20
oceans, 4
predators, 6, 14

prey, 16, 17, 19, 20
range, 4, 5
rocks, 9
seaweed, 9
skin, 8
status, 13
suckers, 10, 17
swim, 15
venom, 19

The images in this book are reproduced through the courtesy of: blickwinkel/ Alamy, front cover (octopus); John_Walker, front cover (coral reef) pp. 2-3; Antonio Martin, pp. 4-5; Michael Ludwig, p. 6; orgbluewater, pp. 6-7, 11; Placebo365, p. 8; David Fleetham/ Alamy, p. 9 (octopus); Chris Holman, p. 9 (coral); Dorling Kindersley ltd/ Alamy, p. 9 (beak); Juniors Bildarchiv GmbH/ Alamy, p. 10 (suckers), 18-19; pr2is, pp. 10-11; Paulo de Oliveira/ Biosphoto, pp. 12, 17; F1online digitale Bildagentur GmbH/ Alamy, pp. 12-13; Media Drum World/ Alamy, pp. 14-15; Rich Carey, pp. 16-17, 21; joesayhello, p. 19 (crabs); Natalia Siiatovskaia, p. 19 (shrimp); Tom Stack/ Alamy, p. 19 (sea cucumber); Julian Gunther, pp. 21-21; Kondratuk Aleksei, p. 22.